Words that are tricky to understand are in **bold**. Find out what they mean in the glossary.

Words that are difficult to say are in *italics*. Find out how to say them at the back of the book.

WHAT IS ROBOTICS?

Robotics is a branch of **engineering** and computer science that involves the idea, design, creation, and operation of robots.

The scientists who study robotics are called **ROBOTICISTS.**

COULD ROBOTS RULE THE WORLD?

DISCOVER THE SCIENCE BEHIND **ROBOTICS**
(roh-BOT-icks)

Written by Eliza Jeffery
Illustrated by Daniel Limon

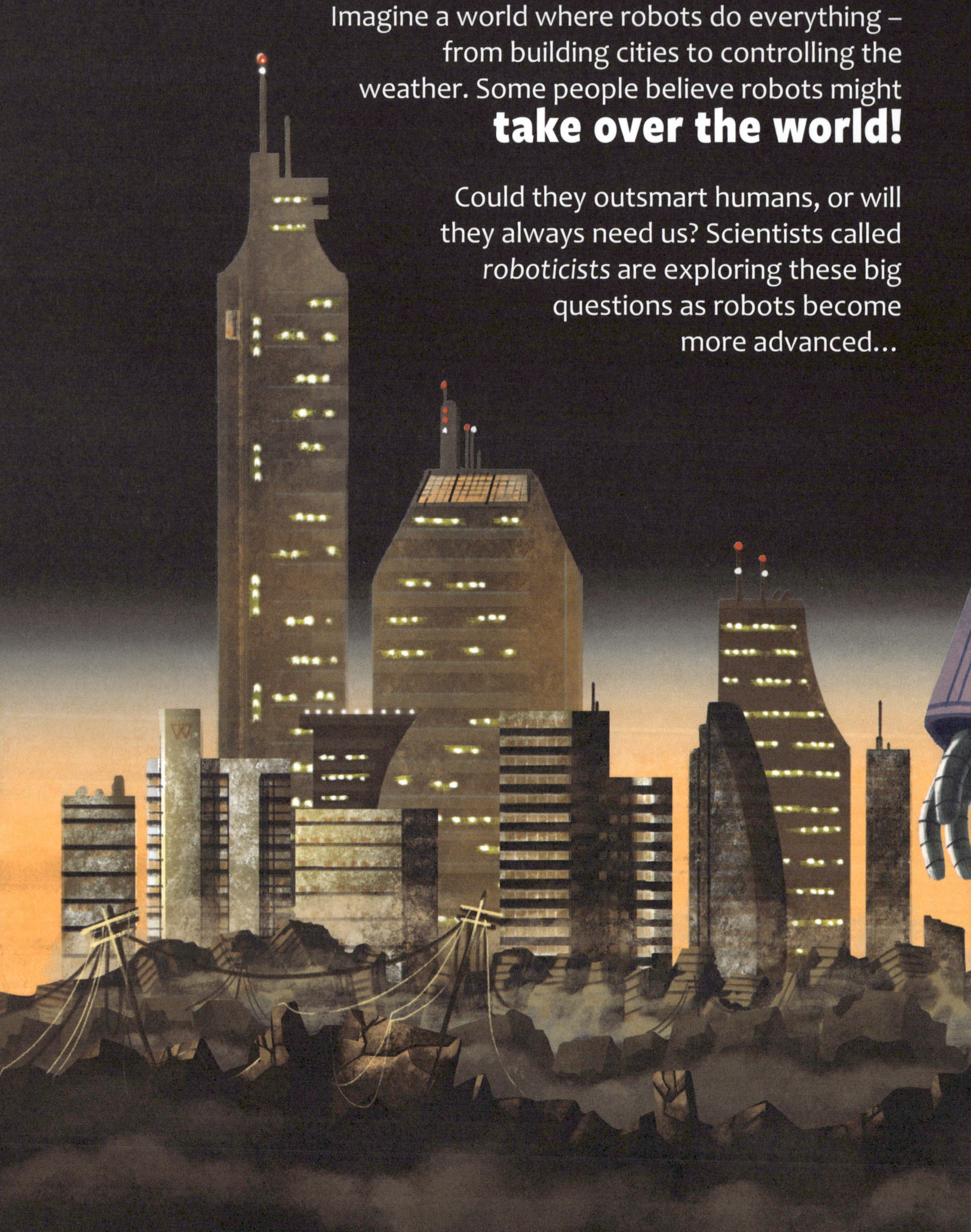

Imagine a world where robots do everything – from building cities to controlling the weather. Some people believe robots might **take over the world!**

Could they outsmart humans, or will they always need us? Scientists called *roboticists* are exploring these big questions as robots become more advanced...

So, what exactly is a robot? The definition of a robot changes as science and technology becomes smarter.

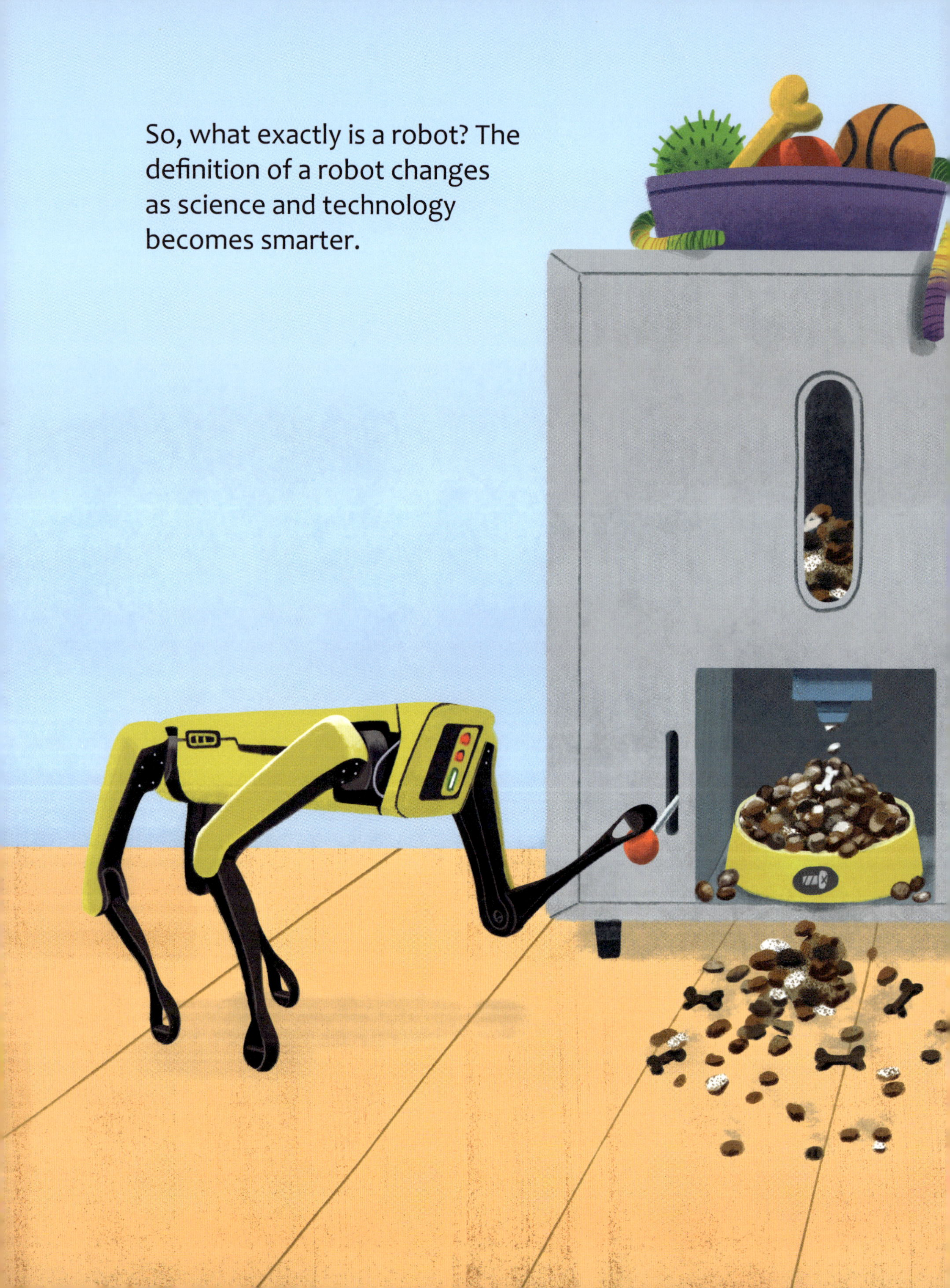

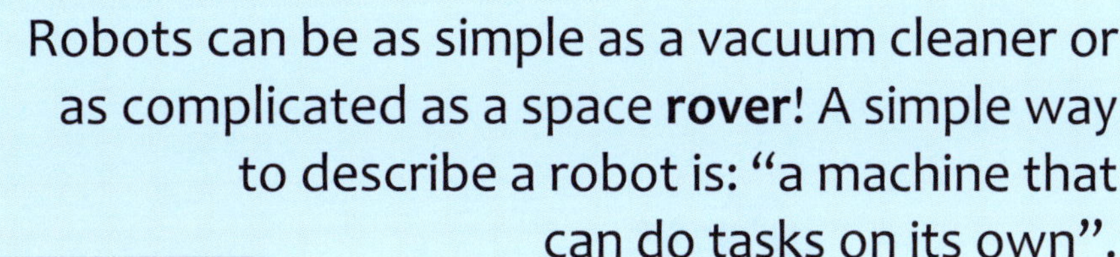

Robots can be as simple as a vacuum cleaner or as complicated as a space **rover**! A simple way to describe a robot is: “a machine that can do tasks on its own”.

Robots are built by roboticists and **engineers**. First, they create the robot's body and add **sensors** to help it detect the world around it. Next, they write **computer code** so the robot can respond and act. It takes lots of teamwork and creativity to

make a robot come to life!

Today, robots are more advanced than ever. Some, like Sophia,
can even hold conversations!

Sophia is a robot designed to look and act like a human. She can make jokes, answer questions, and learn from people around her. This type of robot is called a **humanoid** and it shows just how far robotics has come over time.

Once they're built, robots are ready to get to work! Factories use robots to build large machinery, such as trains and cars...

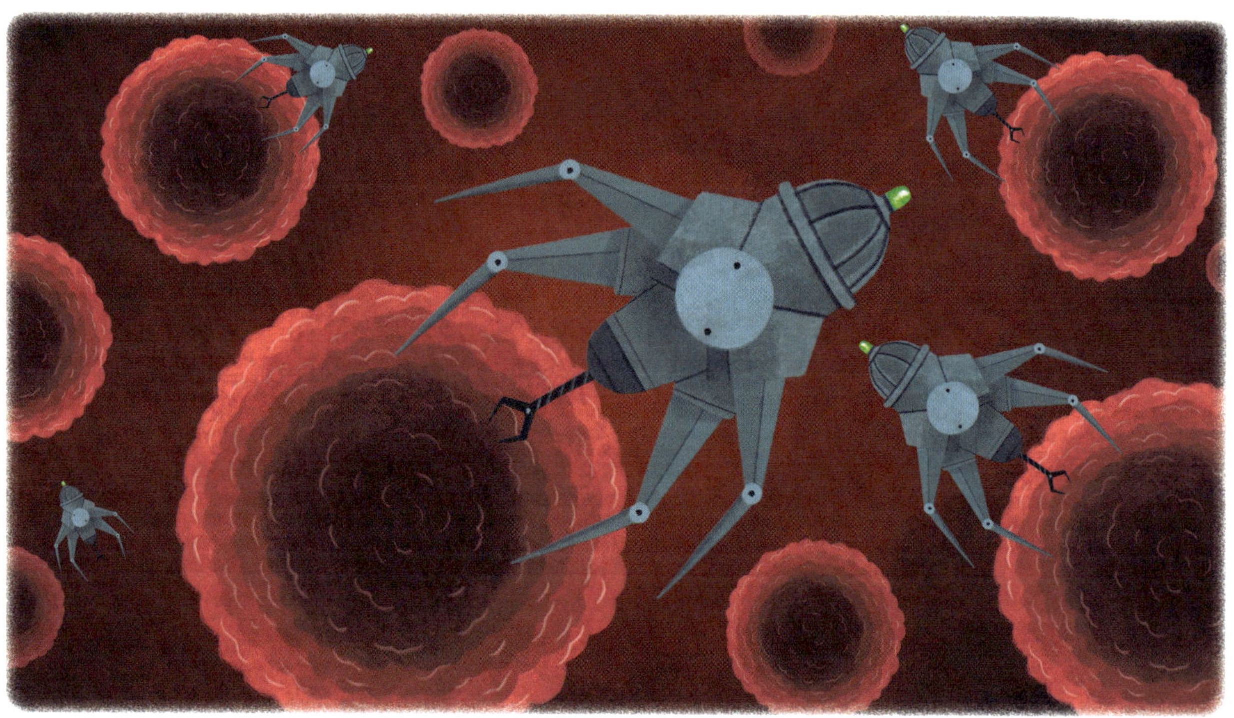

in medicine, tiny robots can be used to treat problems inside the body...

and in times of emergencies, there are even firefighting robots, which help keep humans safe. Robots are fast, strong, and never get tired – a perfect fit for tough jobs!

One amazing robot is Atlas, which is designed to go where humans can't. Atlas can climb, jump, and open doors during rescue missions.

In dangerous situations, like earthquakes or fires, robots like Atlas can search for survivors and deliver supplies, keeping humans out of harm's way.

Robots don't just do incredible things on our planet, but beyond it too. ClearSpace-1 is a robot designed to clean away old **satellites** that float around our planet.

Without robots, this dangerous space junk could harm spacecraft and **astronauts**. Thanks to robots like ClearSpace-1, the future of space exploration is looking much cleaner and safer!

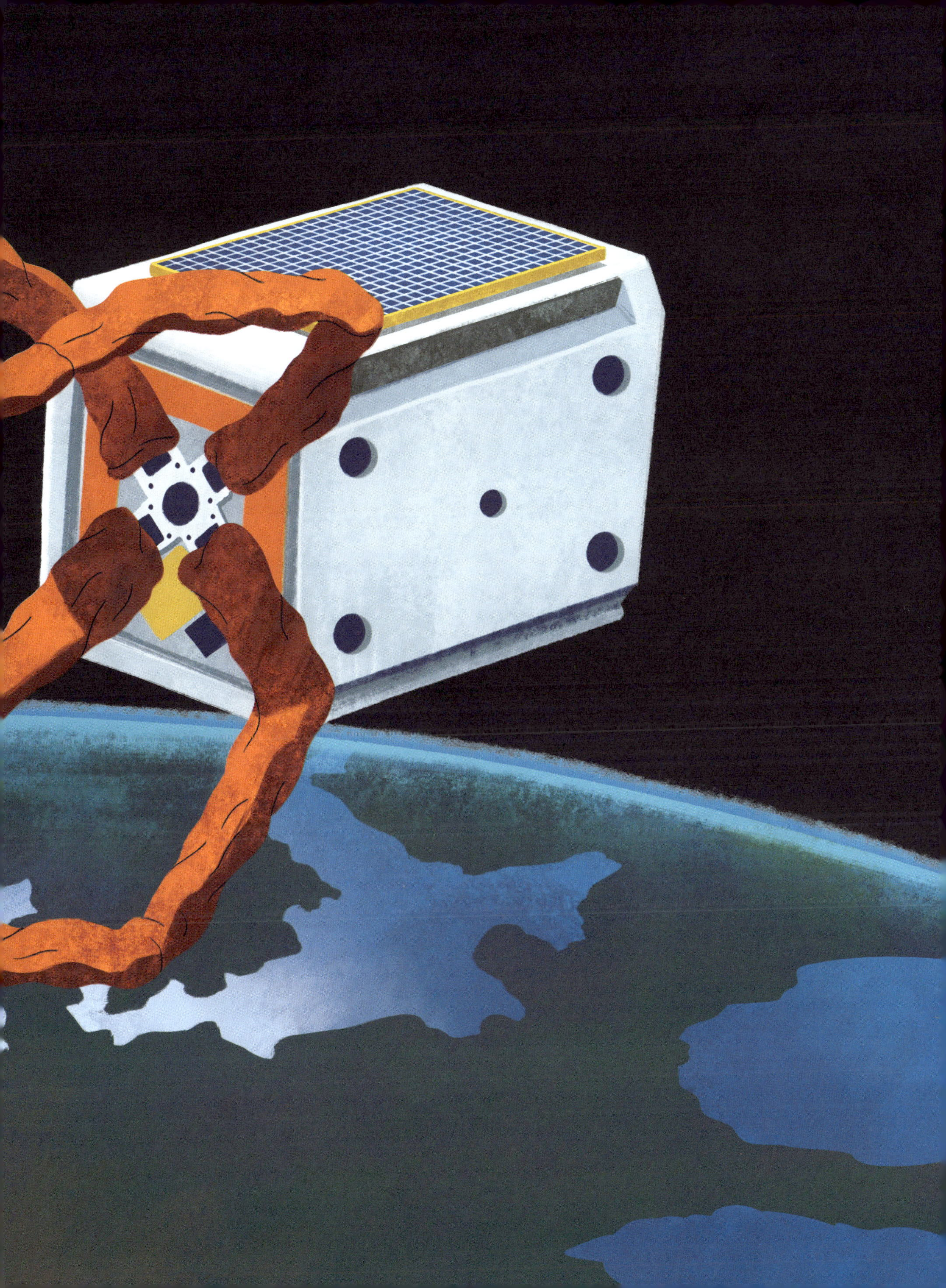

Robots are also helping in nature! One special robot, called SlothBot, hangs in trees to track wildlife and weather changes. Meanwhile, RoboBees are designed to **pollinate** plants and help **ecosystems** thrive.

These clever machines are protecting animals and fighting **climate change,** proving that robots can make a big difference in nature.

What about robots in our busy everyday lives? The CyberCab is a robotic taxi that could transform how we travel. It uses sensors and cameras to **navigate** crowded streets safely, without a human driver!

In the future, robotic cars might make our roads safer and reduce traffic, giving us more time to relax while getting from place to place.

As well as making our lives easier, robots can do very serious things too. In hospitals, robots are **saving lives!**

Surgical robots help doctors perform tricky operations with incredible **accuracy**. They can reach tiny spaces in the body that human hands can't, making surgeries much safer and faster for people.

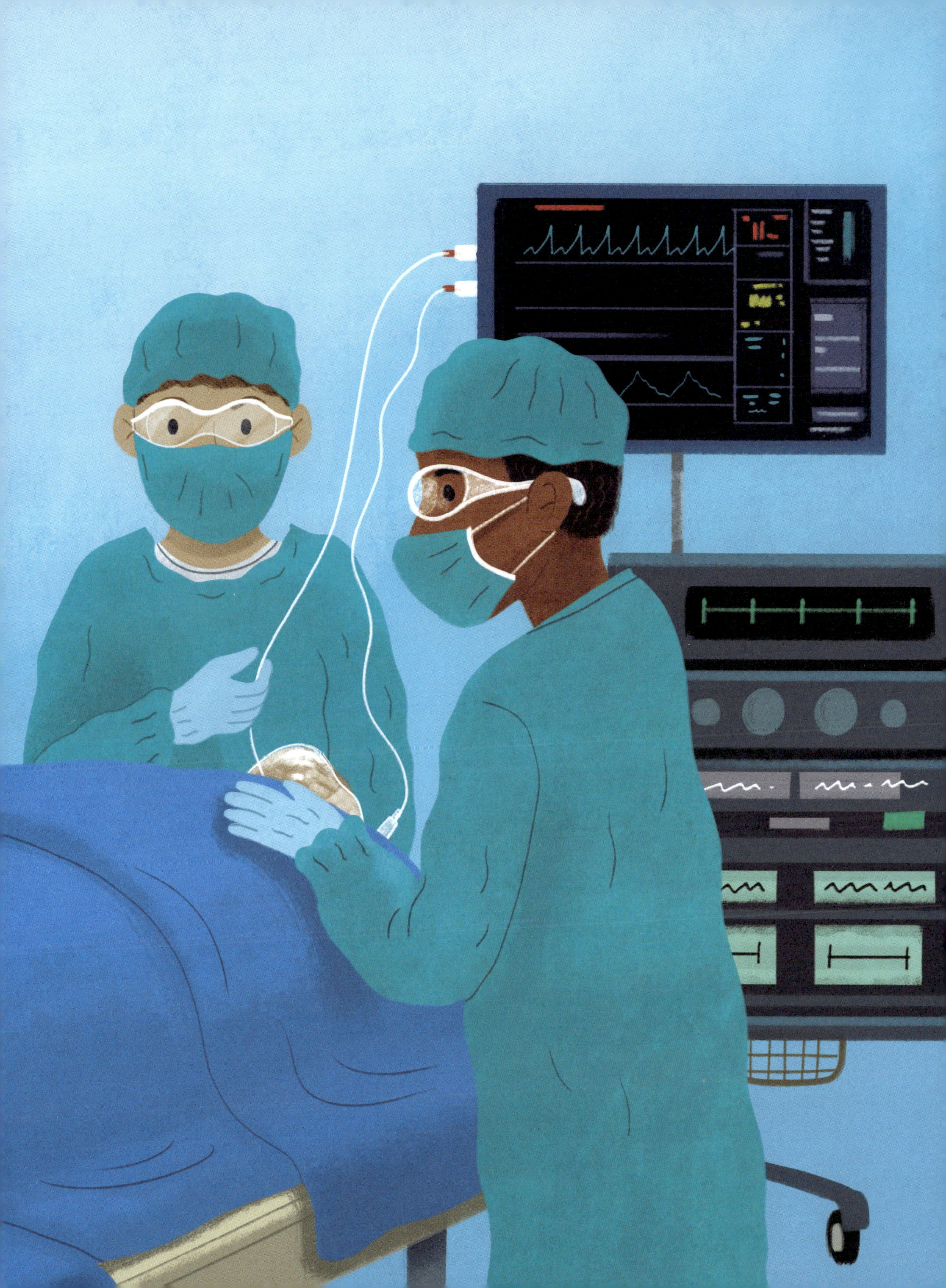

As robots become smarter, people are beginning to ask big questions. Should robots be making decisions? Should they replace human workers? And how do we make sure they are used for the good of humankind?

Scientists are working hard to make sure robots are designed to help, not harm, the world we live in.

The future of robotics is full of endless possibilities. Robots might be able to help us to build homes on other planets one day, or explore what mysteries lie at the bottom of the ocean!

Roboticists are always creating exciting, new ways to use these amazing machines.

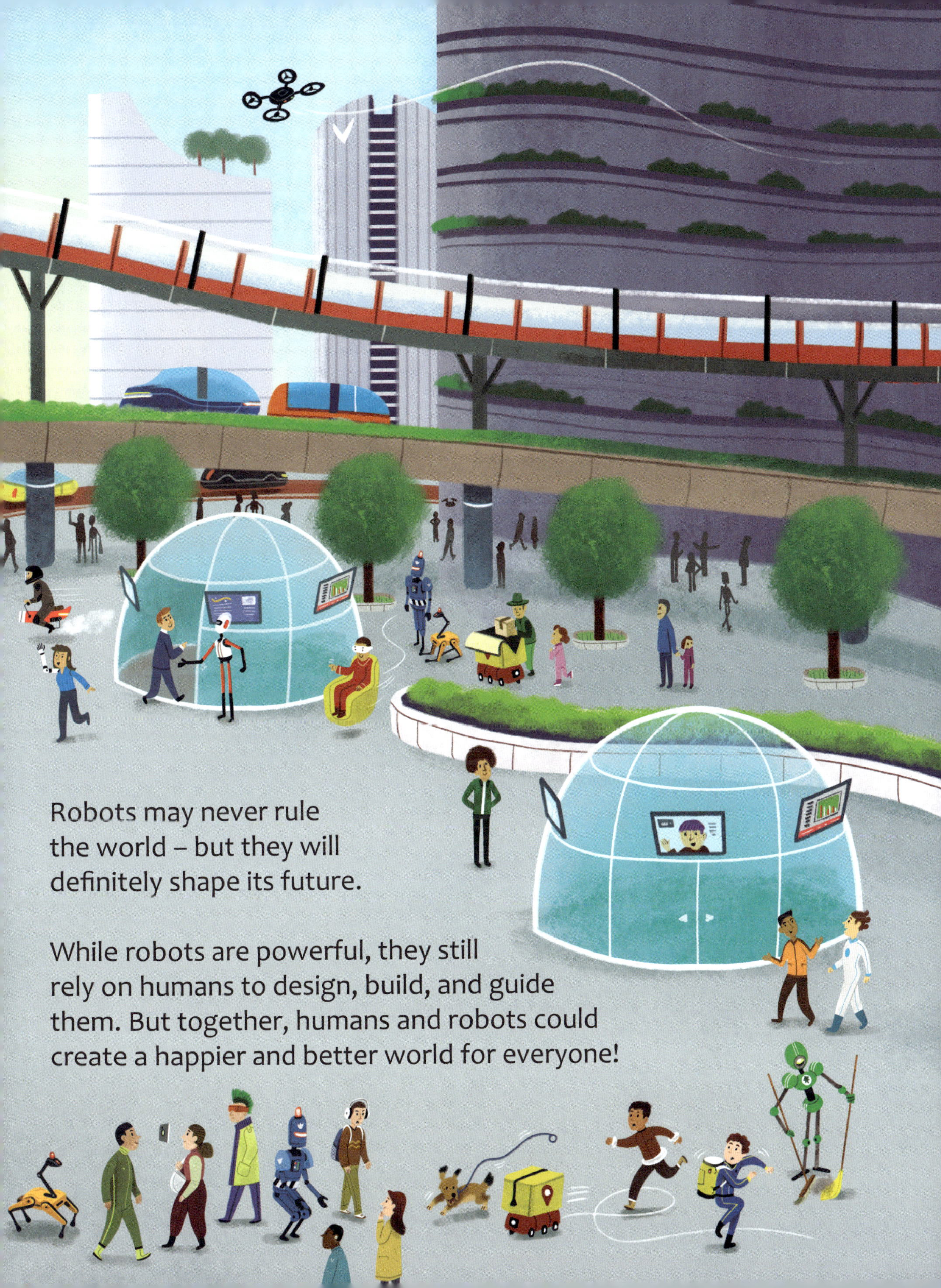

Robots may never rule the world – but they will definitely shape its future.

While robots are powerful, they still rely on humans to design, build, and guide them. But together, humans and robots could create a happier and better world for everyone!

Common types of
ROBOTS

Robots come in all shapes and sizes! Let's take a closer look at some of the most common types of robots and the incredible things they can do.

AUTONOMOUS MOBILE ROBOTS (AMRS)

These machines can perform tasks without human help! They use sensors and **artificial intelligence** to make decisions. AMRs are often found in warehouses and hospitals, moving goods and helping deliver supplies.

AUTOMATED GUIDED VEHICLES (AGVS)

AGVs are robots that transport materials or products in a specific, guided path. Unlike AMRs which can move anywhere, these robots follow tracks or pre-set routes.

ARTICULATED ROBOTS

Articulated robots have mechanical arms that can move in lots of directions, just like human arms! These robots are used in factories, where they perform tasks such as **welding**, painting, and packaging with great speed and accuracy.

HUMANOIDS

Humanoid robots are designed to look and act like humans! They often have two arms, two legs, and a head, but their main purpose is to interact with humans. These are often used in customer service, healthcare, and even act as companions.

COBOTS

Collaborative robots, or cobots, work alongside humans. Unlike some robots that work independently, cobots can interact directly with human workers, making them perfect for jobs that require teamwork!

Remarkable

ROBOT FACTS

There's so much to discover about the world of robotics. Did you know these fascinating facts about robots?

CAN ROBOTS SWIM?

Some robots are specially designed to explore underwater! They can dive down into the ocean to study shipwrecks, coral reefs, and even underwater volcanoes.

WHEN WAS THE FIRST DIGITAL ROBOT BUILT?

The first fully digital robot was built in 1954. It was called "Unimate", and it worked in factories, helping to build cars... and sometimes pour tea!

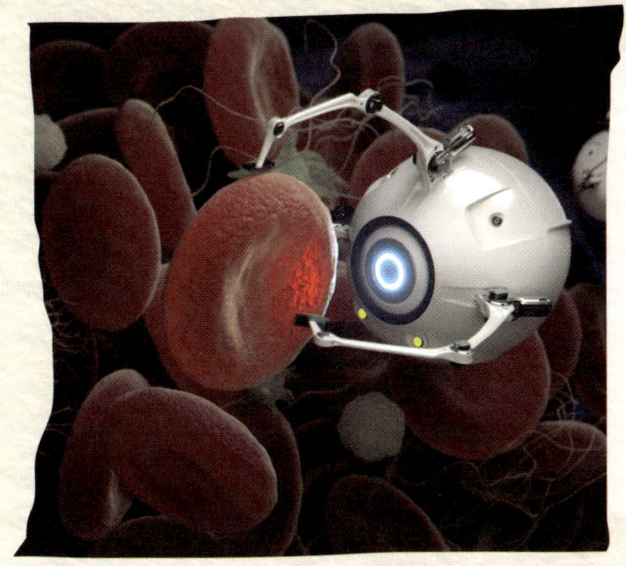

DO TINY ROBOTS EXIST?

Yes! Scientists are building robots so small they can only be seen with a very strong microscope! They are called "nanobots" and will be able to deliver medicine to specific **cells** in the body.

DO ROBOTS ONLY LOOK LIKE HUMANS?

Not all robots look like people! Some are designed to move like animals, such as robotic bees, dogs, and snakes. Maybe everybody will have a pet robot one day!

WHAT IS THE LARGEST WALKING ROBOT?

As of 2024, the largest walking robot in the world is called "Tradinno", a 49-foot (15-m) long dragon. This impressive robot can even breathe fire!

GLOSSARY

Accuracy – being precise and correct.

Artificial intelligence (AI) – the ability of machines to learn and solve problems like humans. *Need help saying this? Look below!*

Astronauts – people trained to travel into outer space.

Cells – the smallest parts of a living thing.

Climate change – a change in the weather conditions over a long time.

Computer code – a special set of instructions that tells a computer what to do.

Ecosystems – all the living and non-living things that exist together within an area.

Engineering – the science of designing and building machines, tools, or systems to solve problems and make life easier.

Engineers – people who use science and creativity to design and build things like robots, bridges, and airplanes.

Humanoid – a robot that is designed to look and act like a human, with features like arms, legs, or even a face.

Navigate – move around.

Pollinate (pollination) – the process of animals helping plants to make seeds by taking pollen from one plant to another plant of the same type.

Rover – a remote-controlled robot that is built to explore extra-terrestrial planets and moons.

Satellites – any object that orbits a planet. Satellites can be natural, like moons, or artificial (made by humans), like the ones we use for communication.

Sensors – special tools on robots that help them detect light, sound, touch, movement, and much more.

Welding – joining two or more parts together, using heat, pressure, or both.

HOW DO I SAY?

Artifical intelligence
ar-tih-FIH-shul
in-TEL-uh-junce

Roboticists
roh-BOT-uh-sists

Robotics
roh-BOT-icks

THE BIG QUESTIONS ANSWERED

This is more than just a series of books; it is a complete resource.
Accompanying each book is a variety of FREE material to engage curious kids with science.

www.thebigquestionsanswered.com

Use the QR code to visit the website, download free resources, and discover other books in the series.

On the website, find out incredible things about roboticists, including what they do, some of their greatest discoveries, and the people who have made a difference in this field of science.

The material is also available for home or classroom use, supporting all the information in this book.

Teachers' & Parents' Resources
With discussion prompts and questions, extra information, and facts around key topics.

Young Roboticists' Activity Pack
Fun activities for wannabe robot experts, including creative writing, drawing, word searches, and much, much more.

The Big Questions Answered is published by Beetle Books.
Beetle Books is an imprint of Hungry Tomato Ltd.

First published in 2025 by Hungry Tomato Ltd
F15, Old Bakery Studios, Blewetts Wharf, Malpas Road,
Truro, Cornwall, TR1 1QH, UK.

ISBN 9781835691458

A CIP catalog record for this book is available from the British Library.

With thanks to:
Editors: Millie Burdett and Holly Thornton
Designers: Amy Harvey and Meg Holbrook
The team at Beehive Illustration
Consultant: Harry Soar

Information in this book is up to date as of the time of writing.

Printed and bound in China.

Picture Credits:
(t = top, b = bottom, m = middle, l = left, r = right)
Shutterstock: ART STOCK CREATIVE 32mr; asharkyu 33tr; FOTOGRIN 32bl; SviatlanaLaza 35mr; Tatiana Shepeleva 35tl; UNIKYLUCKK 33br; VesnaArt 33ml; Vismar UK 34mr.
Wikipedia: By Frank Q. Brown, Los Angeles Times - https://digital.library.ucla.edu/catalog/ark:/21198/zz0002vfhd; By Jevener - Own work, Public Domain, https://commons.wikimedia.org/w/index.php?curid=10866784 35bl.